M000007938

Three
Days changed
Everything

Jase Series Book Three

Written by Jason Crabb
Illustrated by Anita DuFalla

Copyright © 2013 — Jason Crabb Ministries, LLC

All rights reserved. This book or any portion thereof may not be reproduced or used in any manner whatsoever without the express written permission of the author except for the use of brief quotations in a book review. Scripture quotation marked NCV is taken from the New Century Version®. Copyright © 2005 by Thomas Nelson, Inc. Used by permission. All rights reserved.

Printed in the United States of America   ISBN 978-0-9888994-2-1   www.jasoncrabb.com

The JASE Series is dedicated to my girls: my beautiful wife, Shellye,
and our precious daughters, Ashleigh and Emma. You mean the world to me.
With love from our family to yours:
Jason, Ashleigh, Shellye, and Emma.

Special thanks to Philip and Tina Morris and Donna Scuderi for your creative input and love of the cause.

Number
3

The 3rd Commandment

FOR Crabb Kids

Don't be crabby toward God. Say His name with your love.

1. Love God more than all, even crabs great and small.

2. Friend and crab, while you love them, always see God above them.

3. Don't be crabby toward God. Say His name with your love.

4. God's day of rest is for you — and for your crab, too.

5. All children and crabs, respect Mom and Dad.

6. Don't hurt one another, not a crab or your brother.

7. Crab or person alike: love your husband or wife.

8. Never steal from your brother, your crab, or another.

9. Little boys, girls, and crabs, tell the truth and be glad.

10. Be sure to enjoy your stuff and your crab, not wishing for something your neighbor has.

Mateo was happy to find a new friend.
Jase and he met at the supermarket.
Before that Mateo's face was so sad,
but now he laughed at the crab in his bag!

On their way to the car, Jase strummed a song. Mateo and Mami sang along.

As they packed the groceries into the hatch,
Jase bumped into a light that was cracked.

"Oh no!" he said. "My guitar must have smashed it!"

But Mateo knew better.
His eyes filled with sadness.

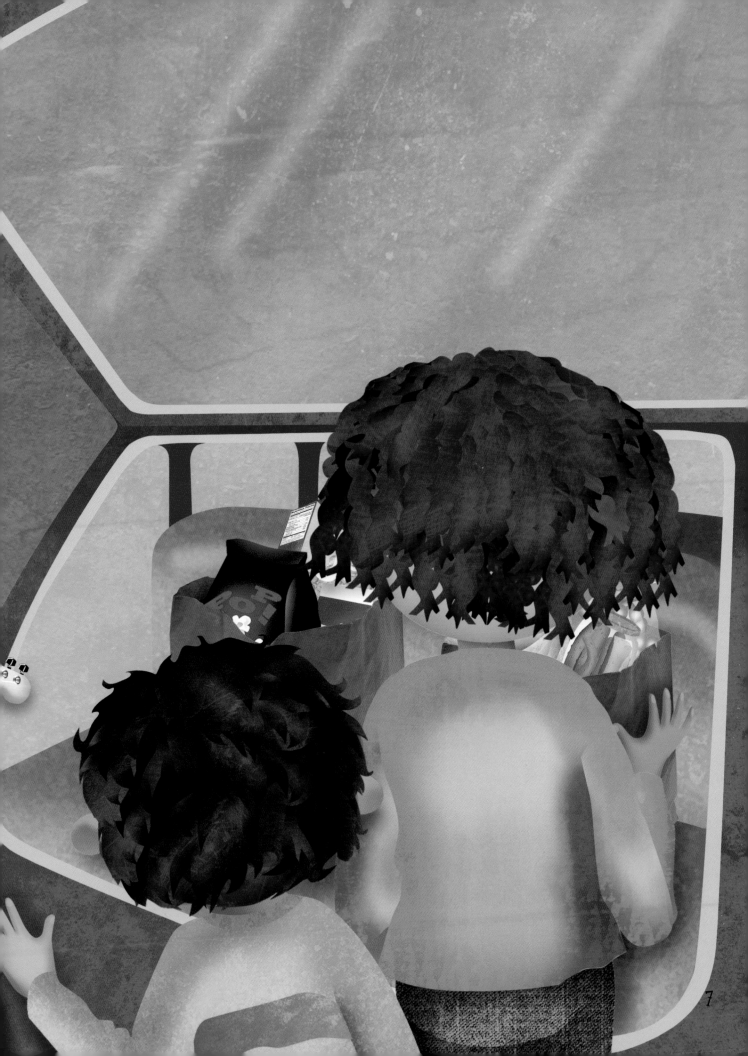

"You didn't break it," Mateo explained.
"It's been smashed for a year and a day.
Papi's company closed, so things have been hard.
Every day he searches for a new job."

"I hope he finds work really soon.
My friends all have bikes and I need one, too.
But there's no money to buy a bike.
So I end up playing alone inside."

"I know what to do," Jase
said. "We can pray!
Often things change in
a matter of days."

"Okay! Let's
pray when we
get home!
But first, Mister
Crabb, put your
seatbelt on."

Back at home, Mateo prayed:
"Papi's interview is in three days."

Jase said, "Lord, it's the perfect time.
In just three days, You saved mankind!"

"Jase? You mean what Jesus did?
To save us from all our sins?"

"Yes, at first His friends were sad,
but three days later, He rose again!"

11

"He tried to prepare them. Let's go and see what He said at their last meal…"

"The Last Supper? Is that what you mean?"

"Yes, Mateo, come and see!"

13

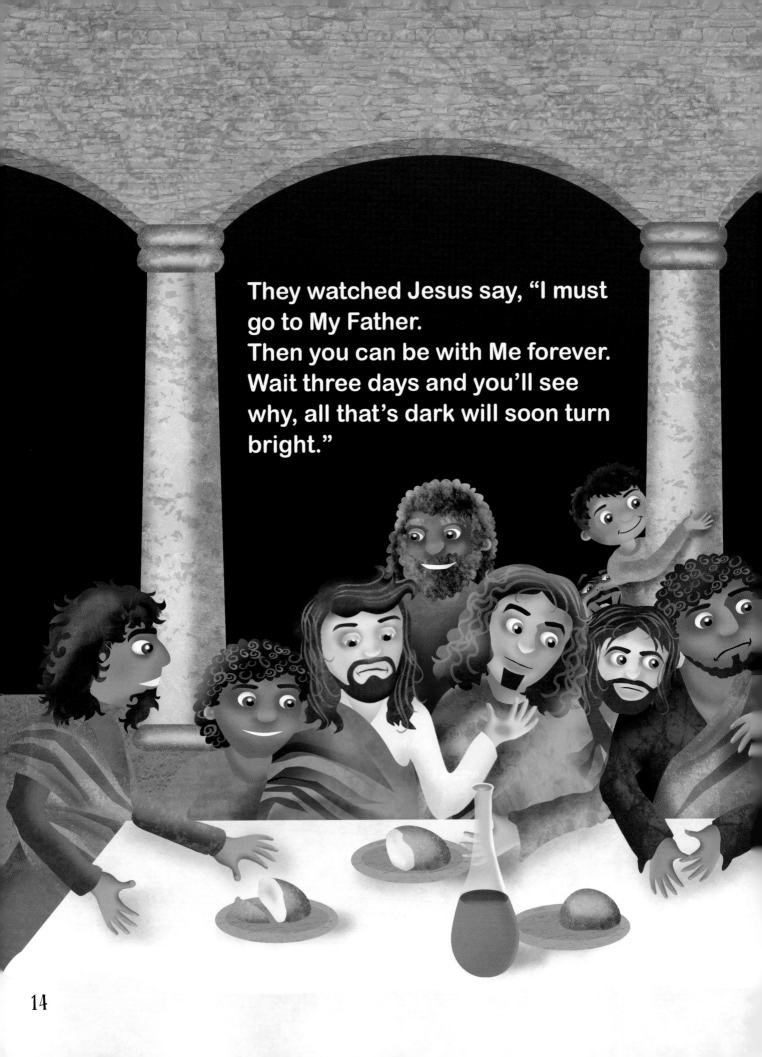

They watched Jesus say, "I must go to My Father.
Then you can be with Me forever.
Wait three days and you'll see why, all that's dark will soon turn bright."

Jase said, "We're about to see the empty grave change everything!"

"Mateo, that's why Jesus came, to bear our scars, but leave the grave.
He rose again so that we could trust in Him, and be set free!"

"Jase, my Papi's in good hands.
Jesus takes good care of him.
He'll find a job. We'll be okay.
Christ already made the way."

"God loved the world so much that he gave his one and only Son so that whoever believes in him may not be lost, but have eternal life" *(John 3:16 NCV)*.

"Right you are! It's time to leave,
to trust, and to wait patiently."

"Let's go inside. Let's get upstairs…"

"Hurry, Jase, three days goes fast!"

"Thank You, Lord, for all You did,
to save us from all our sin.
Now I pray for Papi's job.
Please bless his interview from above."

21

Three days later…

After his interview, Papi said grace,
"Thank You, Lord, for this day…
for the new job You gave me and all that it means
to my precious family."

Mateo leaped, Jase and Mami did, too,
as waves of joy filled the room.

After dinner Papi said,
"I think that we should celebrate,
Let's eat out this Saturday night.
Mateo, what do you have in mind?"

24

"Papi, let's go anywhere,
as long as you are happy there.
But first can we fix our car?
I'll shine it up, bright as a star!"

"Sure we can. I'll help you, son.
I'm proud of everything you've done."

26

"You're never crabby when times are tough.
You only speak God's name
in **love**."

"Papi, you taught me long ago,
to honor God who sees us through."

When Friday came, they got dressed up to celebrate what God had done. Their car was bright and shiny, too. Amazing what three days can do!

Salerno'

While they ate, Jase sang a song.
A girl nearby sang along.
Jase felt a tug upon his heart.
Mateo knew they'd have to part.
He said, "Dear friend, you must leave
and go where God's adventure leads."

Jase smiled and leapt out of his seat.
He had a brand-new friend to meet!

**Jase said, "Well, I guess there's more!
We'll see what happens in Book Four!"**

Jase® — A "Crabb" With a Mission

Children are precious — to us and to God! And their growing-up years are so important to the people they become. Through their everyday experiences, children discover their individual identities, their unique destinies, and the reality of their loving Creator.

When faced with challenges and disappointments, children are comforted to learn that other children share many of the same experiences. As they hear other children's stories, they are strengthened in discovering that they are not alone, or "more strange," or "less courageous" than their peers.

The vision for The Jase® Series took root in my heart two decades ago. Now, as a husband and the father of two beautiful girls, I long to reach children and those who love and care for them with the Good News—the gospel of Jesus Christ! I pray that this children's story will sing the melody of God's heart to you, whatever your age.

— Jason Crabb

coming up next in the Jase series

In this continuing dreamland adventure, Jase and his friend Lily discover that God sends His help wrapped in His love.

Hey kids!

Now that you've read the book, how would you like to:

- Download Jase FUN pages;
- Access the Jase and You Review
- Earn a diploma from Jase University
- And more ...

Go with me to www.jasecrabb.com to continue our journey together!!!